I0141414

Don't Settle For Less Than
What He Has For You

Lesia M. Jones

Copyright © 2007 by Lesia M. Jones
All rights reserved

ISBN # 978-0-6151-5476-3
First Edition

Printed in the USA

Acknowledgements

I would like to thank my Abba Father for not leaving me fatherless.
Thank you to my loving husband, Rev. Edward L. Jones; you are my knight in
shining armor. A special thanks to my daughter, Le'Anne, who spent many hours
editing this work. She also took the picture on the cover. Last but not least, thank
you to my two boys, Jimmie and Jonathan, for their love and encouragement. My
boys always know how to make me laugh!

Table of Contents

From The Author

Let me explain why I am going to share intimate things about my life with you. It breaks my heart to hear people tell of the things this life has dealt them and the affect those things had on their lives. I want them to know that our Lord can and will deliver them from it all if they will let Him. I want them to know that they don't have to settle for less than what He has for them. We do that, you know; we settle for far less than what He has for us.

Just as every good earthly father has an idea of what he wants for his child, our Heavenly Father has a good and perfect will for each of our lives. A good earthly father loves and encourages his child as it grows to accomplish the hopes and dreams of the father, as does God the Father for His children. He is there to love and guide us to accomplish His will for our lives.

I never knew my earthly father, but my Heavenly father always knew me. He knew me before I was formed in my mother's womb. He knew you before you were formed in your mother's womb. In Jeremiah chapter one and verses four and five, the Lord told Jeremiah, "Before I formed thee in the belly, I knew thee" (King James Version). We know that God is not a respecter of persons, so if He knew Jeremiah, He knew you and me!

I was born illegitimately in 1965 to a 19-year-old girl who already had two other babies that were 14 months and 28 months old. It was hard for my mama to bring me into this world as an illegitimate child. I have gratitude in my heart toward her for giving me life. She once told me that she didn't want to keep me at first. I can understand how hard it must have been for her. The encouragement the doctor gave my mama to at least look at me after the delivery caused her to change her mind.

My young mother was divorced from her first husband and was raising her two daughters with very little support from him. When I was born, she had three little girls to raise.

This picture is of Mama's three little girls. I am the one in the middle. Because I was an illegitimate child, I was not accepted by my biological father's family and never received any support from them. Children born in wedlock in his family were taken care of by the family business. They were born heirs into that family, but I was not. When you do not have a daddy here on earth, it is a wonderful feeling to be "chosen." God has adopted me into His family and made me joint heirs with His Son, Jesus Christ, my Savior. He chose me. He chose you.

Chapter One: Childhood Memories

My earliest memories are at about three years of age. These are happy memories of my two half-sisters and me. I didn't realize then that they were my half-sisters; to me they were just my sisters. One happy memory I have with them is sitting on the porch eating our "penny candy" that we bought from the corner store. Mama's boyfriend (at the time) would give us each a quarter to buy a little brown bag of "penny candy." Candy was actually a penny per piece back then. It was sold in individual assorted pieces laid out on a child's eye level to choose from. I can still remember excitedly choosing my pieces and carrying them home in my little brown bag to sit on the porch steps and eat with my sisters.

Other happy memories I have are from the age of about four years old. It was just Mama and her three little girls who had no daddies.

We were living in a little house in Pensacola, Florida, where I was born. Mama had a record player set up in the living room, and I can still hear those old country songs by Loretta Lynn and George Jones blaring throughout the house and out of the open windows. I remember runnin' around barefoot on those wood floors and singing at the top of my lungs with Mama, Loretta, and George. Those are some good memories of Mama smiling. I think Mama played those songs to keep from being sad about her life.

As I think back, it seems that in the early years of my life Mama loved us and wanted a good life for us all, but she didn't know how to make that happen. She didn't let the Lord help her by first giving her heart and life to Him to do with as He wanted. Still, He was there, looking out for me and guiding me so that I would one day have the opportunity to fulfill His will for my life.

‎ℭℜ

When I was five years old Mama met her third husband. This man would become the only "daddy" I ever really had. He would also be the father of Mama's fourth and last child, our little brother. Mama seemed happy when this step-daddy came to live with us. I was not a happy little girl, however, because his arrival meant I no longer got to sleep in the same bed with my Mama. I remember standing at Mama's door whimpering, then hearing that new man's loud, harsh voice say, "You'd better get in that bed!" Gone were the nights when my two sisters and I would all pile into bed with Mama. I remember how on those nights she would lay her heavy legs on ours to make sure we didn't get out of the bed while she was sleeping. I was, therefore, not accustomed to sleeping alone when the new step-daddy arrived, and I didn't go quietly!

I have only one fond memory of when the new step-daddy came to live with us—the smell of fried chicken cooking in the kitchen! I actually smelled it out in the yard and excitedly ran inside, letting the screen door slam behind me. The smell of frying chicken was another thing that I was not accustomed to in our house. Before my step-daddy came, we were living on welfare and commodities.

Commodities were government surplus items that were given to the poor. I think commodities were given before food stamps came along. Commodities were things like powdered milk and eggs, cheese, sugar, peanut butter, and syrup. My sisters and I would mix the peanut butter and syrup up on a plate and eat it. I have a fond memory of us sitting around the table laughing while trying to see who could get it mixed up the quickest. Can't you just see three little girls sitting around the table giggling and feverishly mixing up peanut butter and syrup on a plate?

We rarely had bread. It was a treat when we did. I remember asking, "Mama, can we have a piece of bread?" We asked this question as if bread was a rare treat! We were only allowed one piece each, so we did everything we could to make it last. We first made little bread balls from the bread's center to pop into our mouths, one at a time. Then we took the crust apart, eating each side as if it was a French fry. As another treat, my mama would make coffee for us in tall plastic tumblers. We would put the commodity powdered milk and sugar cubes in it, and boy, was it good!

I think of those days now when my husband and I are volunteering to hand out food to the needy at food banks. My heart goes out to the children I see standing in line with their mama. I remember those days when my sisters and I stood in line with our mama for commodities. We never realized that we were poor. We were happy. I remember laughing a lot then. I had a contagious, deep laughter for a child. I was just happy with myself and wanted everyone else to be happy.

That laughter slowly faded after our step-daddy came. Our lives changed drastically after his arrival. Suddenly there seemed to be this invisible barrier that separated our mama from her three little girls. It was as if his presence and the way that he looked at us when we approached him and our mama created an invisible wall between them and us. It seemed that he wanted Mama separated from us.

CR

Not long after he came, our step-daddy moved our family from the South to the western states to become "fruit tramps." That's what they called us because we lived like tramps while going state-to-state picking fruit. Traveling around from state-to-state picking produce and living "on site" is actually called "seasonal migrant workers."

It was then, in 1972, that our step-daddy's son, our little half-brother, was born. It was also then that this new step-daddy became "Daddy." "Daddy" told my sisters and me that we could call him "Daddy" and that he would be our daddy just like he was to the new baby brother. He said if we started calling him "Daddy" then we would always have to call him "Daddy." However, if we called him by his first name, then we could never call him "Daddy."

I knew I had a real daddy somewhere and I even knew what his name was, but I didn't have him there with me when I was seven years old. I did have this step-daddy who said I could call him "Daddy," so of course I wanted to. I liked the idea of being a real family and being able to call out the word "Daddy" for the first time in my little life. The only thing is, "Daddy" never became a real daddy for me. He was only a "daddy" to his son.

By the time I was eight years old, I had already learned to fear our new "daddy." I also learned to stay out of his way. I knew that he was only in my life because he married my mama and because they had a son together. I knew that his son, my half-brother, was his child and I was not. I knew that he didn't particularly like me and my sisters. I knew this without him ever saying a word. I knew it by the way he looked at me.

We were suddenly not allowed in the house much. We spent most of our days outside while Mama, her new husband, and their new baby sat inside the house. I remember asking to come in because it was hot outside, but he wouldn't let us in where the air-conditioner was. He would lock the door so that we wouldn't bother him.

I remember peeking into the windows of other families' houses and watching the cartoons that the children of that house would be watching. We couldn't hear the sound, but my sisters and I would gather up to the window and watch anyway. I didn't understand why we couldn't sit in our house and watch television like these other children did in their homes—the way we did in our home before the new step-daddy.

Our step-daddy didn't want us around him, our mama, or their new baby. This is when I first began to feel unloved and unworthy. I didn't know it then. I just felt like we were not as good as other children. My step-daddy made me feel that way. I didn't understand why my mama had so suddenly changed. She had never before made us stay outside and away from her.

Children see adults as all-knowing, and they look to them to take care of them. When adults mistreat a child, it instills all kinds of things that the child will have to deal with as they grow up—things like hurt, anger, unworthiness, timidity, and low self-esteem. Adults have power over children to either destroy that child emotionally and mentally or to build that child into a healthy individual. Unhealthy adults sometimes produce unhealthy children.

When I say unhealthy, I mean in emotions, mentality, and spirituality. I hope you can see the importance in becoming the man or woman of God that we need to be, so that we can raise our children up to be emotionally, mentally, and spiritually strong in the Lord.

My step-daddy never said much to me. He never held me and I don't remember him saying that he loved me. I did not know it as a child, but my step-daddy was an alcoholic. I remember in later years watching him put on a pot of coffee in the mornings and having a beer while he waited for the coffee to brew. He would pop the top of the beer and steady himself on the edge of the counter while he downed the whole can without stopping for a breath of air. He would then crush the empty can as if he had conquered it. He was a quiet, inverted, and unhappy man.

That was the first memory I have of my step-daddy's alcohol abuse. I was eight years old, and we were living in a small apartment in Mecca, California, waiting to begin the "fruit run." There were three little twin-sized beds, for my two sisters and me, all lined up in the only bedroom the apartment had. Mama, our new daddy, and our baby brother shared a bed that pulled out from the couch in the living room. The apartment had one small bathroom and a small kitchen. I can remember everything about that little apartment. It was there that I had some of the saddest and hardest times of my childhood. It was there that I remember feeling God's Holy Spirit for the first time. It was the there that I realized that I was a sinner and I needed Him.

Chapter Two: The Age of Accountability

It usually takes a life-altering event in a person's life, one that is beyond what the person can handle, to cause their heart to reach out for understanding and reasoning. At eight years old, the event that was beyond what I could handle was my mama's accident and the fact that she was so suddenly taken away from me. She didn't die, but had been involved in an accident that required a long hospital stay.

Being only eight years old, I didn't realize what was going on. I knew that it was serious and that Mama could have been killed. The realization came to me that if she had died she would not have gone to Heaven. While I was still living in the South my Sunday school teacher, who was also my grand maw, taught me what sin was and how it would keep me from getting into Heaven. I knew that my mama had sinned.

I suddenly realized that I could die at any time, and I was not sure if I would go to Heaven or not. As parents, we need to remember that our children will start to feel conviction at a young age and we need to be sensitive to the Holy Spirit when raising them. Mama had not taught me about the things of God, but instead left it up to my grand maw to teach us.

I thank God for my grand maw. She spent time with me as a child and took me to church. She taught me about Jesus. Grand maw saw me through the eyes of Jesus. She saw me as a legitimate child of God and I felt clean and worthy with her because of the love of Jesus that I felt. I was so young that I didn't realize that it was Him that I felt. I didn't realize that it was Him that made me feel clean and worthy and loved.

ဢ

Grand maw wasn't with me when I was eight years old in Mecca, California, but the Holy Spirit that filled her was. I lay in my little twin-sized bed, the third in a row of three, and whispered with my sisters about what had happened during the day of my mama's accident. We were afraid to talk in front of our step-daddy earlier that day, so we waited until bedtime.

Lying there in our little beds, the middle sister and I began telling our older sister how our step-daddy was late picking us up after school. We didn't think a lot about it at first, because when he arrived he was smiling out of the passenger-side window of his friend's car. He was drinking a beer and talking to his friend as if nothing was wrong.

Getting into the car, my sister told my step-daddy of a minor injury she had acquired that day, which was not unusual because she acquired one most every day. My step-daddy laughed and said, "I guess I will have to take you to the hospital with your mama." Needless to say, he had my attention!

My step-daddy wouldn't explain anything to us, and that frustrated me. He just kept laughing and talking to his friend while they drank beer and drove us home. I could not understand why he was laughing if my mama was in the hospital. I had never felt so scared, confused, and angry. I didn't know it then, but now that I look back on the situation, I honestly think my step-daddy was scared, too. For the first time in his life he had four kids to take care of on his own. I really don't think he knew what to say to us, so he drank his beer and didn't say anything at all.

ᘓ

I look back on the family I grew up with—my mama, my step-daddy, and my brother and sisters—and I can see just how pitiful we all were. A family without God does not know how to be a family. My husband preaches today that the man is the head of the household and needs to line up with the Word of God. He says that if the man lines up, it will be easier for the wife to submit to the Word and to be the wife and mother that the Word teaches her to be. Together, the parents are to raise the children up in the Lord.

Because of my family situation, I always felt like everybody else was better than we were—better than I was. For one reason, my real daddy didn't want me, and my new daddy didn't want me because I wasn't his. For another reason, I was the "other sister." Because my two older half-sisters shared a daddy and a mama, it was always said that they were "real sisters." Although we all shared a mama, we all knew that I had a different daddy and there seemed to be an invisible divider between them and me—separating me as the outsider.

My sisters were always closer to each other than they ever were with me, and I had to accept it through the years. I always wanted to be "part of them" but I seemed to be "set apart" at an early age.

CR

Getting back to the night of my mama's accident, I remember my sisters and me lying there in our three little beds in a row and the oldest sister telling what had happened to our mama that day. The oldest sister had stayed home from school and was with Mama. She said that Mama, our step-daddy, our little brother, and two other people were all involved in an automobile accident. All six were in our old car when my step-daddy slowed the vehicle and attempted to make a left-hand turn off a two-lane road without signaling. An eighteen-wheeler attempted to pass the slowing car, smashing into the back of it when my step-daddy turned into the truck's path. Mama was in the back where the truck rolled onto the car.

I lay there in my bed listening and realizing that my mama could have died. I had learned from my grand maw in our Sunday school class that if we did bad things we would not go to Heaven. I knew my mama drank a lot, smoked cigarettes, and used curse words, and I was afraid that if she died she would not go to Heaven.

To a small child those things are "big sins." Now that I am grown and walking with God, it concerns me to hear Christians harp on those "big sins" and never mention the sins of the heart. "Pineapples and Oranges" is one of my husband's sayings. "It's all the same to God."

We all know that there is no little sin or big sin. Sin is sin and we have all sinned! Romans 3:23 says, "For all have sinned, and come short of the glory of God" (King James Version).

Thank God that "His mercy and compassions are new every morning!" (King James Version, Lam. 3.23). In the eyes of the world we can be the sweetest people and do the most wonderful things, yet still be as filthy rags in the eyes of God. The word of God says, "...there is none that doeth good, no, not one" (King James Version, Rom. 3.12). Not until God makes you into a child of His own, by the precious shed blood of His son Jesus Christ, are we anything. Not until we fall on our face and repent before God, confessing that we are nothing and can be nothing except through the blood of His son Jesus, can we enter into Heaven and escape Hell.

I have heard it said that God will not send us to Hell because he is a loving God. Those who say this are right. He is a loving God and He does not send anyone to Hell; we send ourselves. We don't get saved just for a ticket into Heaven and to escape Hell after we die. We are saved to have the relationship with God that He desperately desires for us to have. We are saved to have peace and love in life instead of hurt and grief. We are saved for others and not just for ourselves. Now there's an idea! The very thought that we are not the only reason that we need to be saved! Who would have thought of it that way—it is not just about us!

◌

I went to sleep the night of my mama's accident scared and desperate-feeling. Our little apartment in Mecca was quiet. Everybody just waited for Mama to come home from the hospital.

We no longer had a car. It was totaled in the wreck, so my aunt came to take us to see our mama. We couldn't go into the hospital. Back then they didn't let children inside. Instead, my aunt took us to the window outside of my mama's room so my mama could wave to us through the window. As she began to get well, she was able to come into the visiting room to see us. I always hated saying good-bye when it was time to go. I remember feeling like the whole world was crushing in on my little chest. I decided in my heart that it was okay if I did have to share my mama with my step-daddy and baby brother. I just wanted my mama back home with me.

Up until that point, I had not forgiven my step-daddy for putting me out of my mama's bed, and though I loved my baby brother, I still had not forgiven my mama for bringing him home from the hospital. I soon decided that I could live with those things if I could have my mama back. I have done that in my adult life, too. I figure out what is important to me and I force myself to do what I have to in order to make it happen. I could not do it without the Lord's help. We change when we are forced to. What I mean by being "forced" is that the condition of our heart causes our flesh to change, and that's a good thing.

We didn't have much food in the house while Mama was in the hospital. I remember my step-daddy laying out some bread and ketchup on the counter and telling my sisters and me to make a ketchup sandwich. I remember looking into his face as he said, "I'll try to get y'all something better later. Maybe your mama will come home soon and things will get better around here." He had such a sad look in his eyes. I really feel that he felt bad for us because we were hungry and needed our mama. It was the first time, and one of the few times, that I felt like maybe he liked us and that maybe he had been talking to God, too.

Every night after my mama's accident I lay in my little bed and cried. I whispered to my sisters that if we weren't good we would not go to Heaven when we died. I look back now and see the awesome thing that God was doing in me. A little eight-year-old girl was crying out to warn her sisters while being under the conviction of her own sins. God was all over me night after night as I wept.

Chapter Three: Needing a Real Father

Mama finally came home from the hospital. When she was well enough, we set out on the "fruit run." We lived in tents and campers during this time. My sisters and I were always separated from Mama, our step-daddy, and our little brother. It was always the three of them in a camper or tent and we three girls in the back of a truck camper shell or in the back of a station wagon. We used outhouses and bathed under faucets or in rivers. It was kind of fun at first, but it got old after a while.

It was at this time of my life that I have an awful memory of my step-daddy throwing me out into the deep water of a river and saying, "swim or sink!" I sunk! I remember the awful feeling of panic that no one was going to help me, and I could not help myself. I was going down for the last time when I caught a glimpse of my mama sitting on the shore. Before going under I heard my step-daddy laughing as he watched from just out of my reach. He finally reached down, grabbed me, and threw me to the shore. I remember sitting there, with my knees drawn into my chest, sobbing.

It was around this time that I began having the feeling in my heart of wanting someone to "come get me." One of my favorite ministers, Bishop T.D. Jakes, once gave a message about this very subject. His message was titled "Help Is On The Way." Bishop Jakes discussed a feeling that abused and neglected children sometimes get of "wanting someone to come and get them." As I listened to him preach, I remembered feeling that way as a child. I remember going off by myself a lot and finding somewhere to sit and cry. I would cry and talk to my real daddy who I hoped was in Heaven listening to me and would somehow send me help. I imagine now that God listened with a grieving heart because He knew that I didn't know that I could cry to Him like that.

ଓ

My real daddy was killed when I was nine years old, and I felt an overwhelming loss for this daddy that I never got the chance to meet.

My grandmother sent us the newspaper clipping announcing his death, and when I read it I sat holding onto that little piece of paper sobbing. I had yet to see a picture of my real father, so I didn't even know what he looked like except that I supposedly looked just like him. I didn't even have his name. I had the last name that my mother carried at the time that I was born. It was the last name of the father of my two half-sisters.

My two sisters always got cards and presents from their father's family, but I didn't. I knew by the age of four that their daddy was not my daddy, and I was different. I always yearned for my daddy and the cards and presents that they got from theirs. After my grandmother sent me the newspaper clipping of his death, I knew that I wouldn't get presents from my daddy or even get to know him.

I remember when my two sisters were reunited with their real father in their adult lives. They introduced me to their father as their sister, but he and everyone else knew that I was not his daughter. I looked away and to the ground to conceal the bitterness and humiliation that I was feeling. I felt so out-of-place.

I was happy for them, but I didn't want to take part in their special day. I was glad that they were able to meet their real daddy, but it made me feel like the "bastard child." Mama was there, but offered me no comfort. I didn't know what to do with all of the feelings that were overwhelming me. I just needed to get away...so I ran.

That is how I had learned to deal with emotion—run. God had to teach me a better way as I got older in the Lord. He taught me, in my time alone with Him, to let Him help me to deal with the things in my life. By doing so, I would be able to handle my emotions without running. I had been running from my childhood and my step-daddy long enough. As an adult I would still have dreams of running away from my step-daddy and my mama. I finally quit running after facing up to, and letting God heal me of, my childhood.

CR

There were a lot of times that I wanted to run away as a child. My step-daddy worked us hard, but it still seemed like we never had anything. We never had a real home or enough food. We moved around frequently and lived mostly in a camper on the back of a truck or in tents.

Mama and our step-daddy sat up most nights drinking by the campfire after putting us to bed. We had to rest up for the next day of work.

My step-daddy would get us up the next morning at six and tell us to "get after it." I remember wondering why Mama didn't come wake us. I just knew she would be kinder in the way she woke us compared to the harsh way that our step-daddy did. I wanted my Mama.

I wanted Mama to come with us, but sometimes Mama would sleep and wouldn't come out until it was time to bring our lunch. I was always glad to see her. My step-daddy didn't speak quite as harshly to us when she was around, and I felt a little safer. Lunch was also the only time we were allowed to stop working, except for trips to the outhouse—and those were timed. We had a few minutes to eat, and then it was back to work. My mama and step-daddy would spend time sitting under a tree or visiting other parents in the field and leave us to do the work. I never understood that.

Now that I am older I still can't understand how parents can use their children to make a living instead of making a living for their children. It is not our children that owe us a living, but we as parents that owe it to our children. The word of God says, "... for the children ought not to lay up for the parents, but the parents for the children" (King James Version, II Cor. 12.14).

When my sisters and I picked cherries we had buckets strapped around our shoulders and back. We were so little that we would fall off the ladders when we would pull on a limb that was heavier than we were. The limb would go back to its original position with us hanging on! I remember falling off my ladder several times, then running around frantically trying to catch my breath. My step-daddy would laugh from his position under one of the trees and tell me to get back up the ladder and get to work.

Other fruits that my sisters and I picked on the fruit run were apples, oranges, lemons, grapefruit, peaches, and grapes. I remember getting into a lot of trouble when we picked apples. I was too little to carry the long apple bag we used, and it would drag and bruise the apples I had picked. I also remember battling the cold when we picked the apples. We went to Washington for apple-picking, a state so cold that we had to put plastic over our socks before putting on our shoes so that our feet would keep warm.

CB

I remember Mama telling my sisters and me that working hard would teach us how to be good workers. Now that I am an adult I have my own opinion about that philosophy. Working hard did teach me endurance, but I am a good worker because I choose to be. My definition of being a good worker is not necessarily connected to grueling physical labor.

I believe a family should work together and share chores, but I don't believe a child should be responsible for their food or the income of the family. If we girls ever complained about working, my mama and step-daddy would ask, "You want to eat don't you?" Those words still ring in my ears today as I stand in my kitchen preparing food for my family.

We need to realize that our children will remember the hurtful comments that we make to them. I don't want to tear my children down or hurt them by the few moments of frustration that I may have with daily responsibilities and struggles. I don't want them having things to deal with later in life because of something I said while I was frustrated. There have been several times when I have had to go to my children and ask for their forgiveness because I flew off the handle and let garbage shoot out of my mouth.

God will teach us to have a good relationship with our children through the relationship that we have with Him. We need to speak to our children the way we want our Heavenly Father to speak to us. You will know when our Father speaks to you. He will always come in love and encouragement.

CⱰ

I remember when our step-daddy whipped us. He would laugh when we cried. He enjoyed making fun of how we reacted to his whippings. A real father would never laugh at his children after whipping them. Our Heavenly Father would never discipline us that way. If you ever feel condemned or ashamed, it is not from God! God corrects us and disciplines us with love, and then he gently picks us up and encourages us to go on. Make sure you understand this. The Devil loves to disguise himself as our Heavenly Father to condemn us and make us ashamed so that we will fall away and turn from God. Don't ever fall for his lies.

Satan is the accuser. When he comes to you and reminds you of your faults and failures or of the past you had before coming to the Lord, remind him of his future!

CⱰ

Mama never whipped us like my step-daddy whipped us. She left all the whipping to him after she married him. Every once in a while she would step in, when he would get carried away, and tell him it was enough. There were times when I thought that if she didn't say something he was going to beat the breath completely out of me. I always gave him a good fight, though. I hated going around with whelps on my back, arms and legs. Those whelps made me feel that anyone who saw them would think I was a bad girl.

My step-daddy also used any excuse to whip us, and he whipped us hard. There was never any loving discipline for us or loving instruction. My step-daddy used his belt, his eyes, and his remarks to turn three happy little girls into three scared, sad, and troubled young ladies.

Chapter Four: Grand Maw

When I was eleven years old we stopped the fruit run and returned to Alabama. I was glad to move back home where Grand maw was. My grand maw was a good grandmother to me and I felt special when I was with her. Grand maw would pick me up to stay with her after we came back from California, and those are some of the most precious memories I have of her. I want to devote this short chapter to my grand maw and to those special memories.

One memory I have is of pretty lacy dresses that she would sew for my sisters and me. Those things must have taken hours to make, because I remember pageant-style dresses hanging up for us to wear on Easter Sunday, with pretty little panties and slips to go with them.

My grand maw also made dolls for us with bodies made of socks and yarn for their hair. Their faces were painted on and they had slips and panties just like the ones made for us. Their dresses where beautifully made, just as ours were. Grand maw loved us, and it showed.

I remember going to church in Grand maw's old LTD. We would travel in it down old country roads to get to her church. I would stand up in the seat beside Grand maw with my head sticking out of the sun roof singing, "Ain't Gonna Need This House No Longer" with Wilma Lee and Stony Cooper on an old eight track tape player that she had in her car. All the while Grand maw would be smiling and pulling on my dress hollering, "You better get down here before you eat some bugs!"

I have sweet memories of going after church with Grand maw to a little old-fashioned hamburger stand and getting huge cheeseburgers. We would take them back to her house and get out all of her gospel records and listen to them while we ate those cheeseburgers. Grand maw would also sit down and read the Bible to me. She helped me to understand things in the Bible and about life.

☙

My grandmother's home was so sweet. It was a small home, but it was precious. Grand maw had crochet blankets and home-made pillows on her chairs and couches. She had pictures on her walls of Jesus holding little children.

Her house had two bedrooms, but Grand maw would always let me sleep with her in her big, soft, tall bed. It seemed to me that she had three or four mattresses on her bed, because I had to use a step-stool to climb in. That bed and her entire house smelled sweet and clean. I would wiggle around in her big soft bed thinking that I was the luckiest little girl alive. I smile to myself when I remember her saying to me, in her sweet voice, "I wish you would hurry up and get your nest made." I would giggle and could almost hear her smiling. I felt safe and loved.

ᲪᲜ

Waking up at my grand maw's house was so nice. I remember my grand maw getting up in the mornings and reading her Bible out loud. I would lie in bed listening to her as she would pray for me and everybody in her family by name before she was done. It was always a deep groaning prayer that would rip your heart out to hear. It stirred my little heart. I would never get up until I knew that she was finished. It felt like a sacred time, and I didn't want to interrupt her and God as they talked.

When I did get up, Grand maw would make me oatmeal with milk and brown sugar. We shared breakfast together at her little table where she had her Bible spread out. I miss those days and my grand maw. I think of her every single time that I make oatmeal with milk and brown sugar for my children.

❧

These memories are from the ages of 11-15. As you will read in the next chapters, I was moved back to California at the age of 15 and didn't come home again for another four years. By then I was grown and didn't get to spend as much time with my grand maw as before.

My grand maw was getting old and was being moved around to different family members. She was not herself in the last few years of her life. She suffered with Alzheimer's disease in her last days and didn't act like the Grand maw that I knew growing up. I know that when she was in her right mind she loved and served Jesus. There were things, times, and people that she did not remember, but she always remembered me. The last time that I saw her alive, my mother asked her, "Mama, do you know who this is?" My grand maw replied, "Why yes, that's my Lesia."

My grand maw passed away in 1996 and I felt like a part of the little girl in me died, too. I know she prayed for me as a child to help me get through a hard childhood. I know Grand maw prayed me into the family of God. She was a big part of me becoming a Christian.

After she died, I got out the last birthday card that she had signed for me. She would always write, "Love, Mo" on all of her letters and cards to me. Her handwriting was all squiggly, and I could just imagine her sweet old hand shaking while she wrote with a loving look on her face.

When Grand maw's things were being divided up within the family, Mama asked me what I wanted. I told her that all I wanted was that old eight track tape of Wilma Lee and Stony Cooper because it held my fondest memories of my grand maw. At thirty years old, I yearned for the times I had with my Grand maw when I was younger. I missed the times that I would sit at her feet and just listen to her talk.

Chapter Five: Unworthiness

I don't know the real reason we moved back to Alabama when I was eleven years old. I do remember that the authorities had begun strict enforcement of the child-labor laws in the fruit fields right before we left California. I still remember officials storming the fields and my step-daddy hollering at us to get our buckets off and sit down so that it would appear that we were not working. It was at this time of my life that I began to feel that my step-daddy had no use for us unless we were working to earn our keep.

അ

I actually had somewhat of a normal life for a few years when we returned to Alabama. We lived in a house and had a garden in which we all worked. We had nice fresh vegetables on the table, and Mama learned to make homemade biscuits. My sisters and I wanted to be in the kitchen with her when she was cooking, and she didn't seem to mind. However, if our step-daddy was home he would say, "Get out of there and leave your mama alone!" He seemed to be very jealous of our mother and her relationship with us. He didn't like us being around Mama or him. If we were sitting in the same room with him, he would tell us to get in the floor or out in the yard where we "belonged." We were not allowed to sit on the furniture if he was home. If my mama was in the room, we were not allowed to sit by her or love on her in his presence. He would say, "Get up from there and leave your mama alone."

When my mama and step-daddy had company over and one of us walked into the room, my step-daddy would point his finger at us with his eyes closed and an "I mean it" look. We knew this meant to get out and stay out. I remember feeling so disappointed when Mama would not take up for us. Her silence made me feel like she chose my step-daddy and others over us. She had changed and I missed the mother of my toddler days.

CR

I remember feeling forsaken, cast aside and worthless by this time of my life. God's Word says in Psalms 27:10 that when our father and mother forsake us, the Lord will take us up. He makes us feel special. He has time for us. He longs to spend time with us. Nobody is more important or interesting to Him than we are. He will never leave us. He has always been there and always will be.

℈

My mama and step-daddy didn't work regular jobs, so we never seemed to have enough money. I was scared to ask for the things that I needed, because it always seemed to aggravate them. It was hard for me to ask for the personal items that young girls need. I always felt like I was a burden on them. This was a hard area for me to deal with in my Christian walk. God has healed me of the feeling of unworthiness.

I can't tell you the people that I have seen struggle with this in the Church. God is so ready and able to heal and deliver. He showed me that he loved me and that he was more than happy to supply all of my needs. God showed me that when he heard my voice say, "Father,"

He was happy to lean his ear to me and eagerly wait to hear what it was that he could do for me. I can almost hear Him say, "Yes, dear?"

My step-daddy always made me feel that I wasn't worth anything, as if he had to find me things to do to make me worth the air that I was breathing. The morning after he and my mama would have company over, while Mama slept, my step-daddy would make my two sisters and me clean up the beer cans and the stench of soured beer in the house. Then he would tell us once again, with a look of disgust on his face, "Now get out in the yard where you belong."

I really hated it when they would drink on the front porch. When they did, we had to pick up their beer cans as well as their numerous cigarette butts. I would pick up those nasty cigarette butts, one-by-one, on my hands and knees. My step-daddy watched from inside the front door to make sure that every single one was picked up. Hate and anger built up in me—hate and anger that I have had to deal with after coming to the Lord.

All of my step-daddy's words and actions toward me rooted deep into my heart, and only God has been able to heal me and deliver me from the hurt, anger, and unworthiness that they produced. As I write this, I wonder what things in my children's lives will stay with them. I wonder what damage have I done to them. I have tried to raise them better than I was raised, and to be a better parent than what I had, but I know that there have been times that I have failed. I have always made it a point to go to my children and apologize to them when I have failed them. The Lord has helped me to raise my children better than I was raised, but I know that everyone has things from childhood and in life that hurt them. I don't want to hurt my children.

We all have to decide what we are going to do with the hurts and disappointments in life. We can not use them as an excuse to act like we want to, and we can not let them keep us from being the best that we can be. The word of God says in II Corinthians 5:17, "Therefore if any man be in Christ, he is a new creature." If we want to be healed of past hurts, we can no longer act on them. We have to respond as the new creature we are in Christ. We have to respond knowing that we are a child of God.

We are a product of our childhood, but we can not use this as an excuse to be the way that we want to be. God will heal and deliver us if we let Him. We allow Him to do this by learning what His Word has to say and then applying the Word to our lives. I really feel like God is up there rubbing it in Satan's face when we act and respond in a way that is pleasing to God. I can just see Him holding the 'ole squirming Devil by the nap of his neck and saying, "Look, Lucifer! Look at my child. That's my child!"

଎

I don't really know what happened between my mama and my step-daddy, but they separated after ten years of marriage. My mama decided that she wanted to move away from Alabama with a new man. I was fifteen and my little brother was eight when my step-daddy left. I was glad to see my step-daddy go, but I felt bad for my little brother because I knew what it meant to want your daddy in your life.

After my mama and step-daddy divorced, I didn't see my step-daddy again until I was 28 years old. I saw him in a whole new way. I saw him for the sad man that he was, and I was not afraid of him anymore. He died when I was 31 years old, and I cried.

Just a few days before he died, I went to see him in the hospital. He was yellow from the poison that alcohol had produced in his body and had slipped into a coma. He had literally drank until he was at the point of death. I leaned down into my step-daddy's face and told him

44

that Jesus loved him, and asked him to call out to Him. I did not want him to feel alone and scared. I didn't want him to feel unworthy like he had made me feel all of my childhood. I forgave him inside my heart and I prayed for him. A tear fell down his face and tears fell down mine.

I did not want this man to go to Hell, even though he had put me through hell as a child. I loved him after all. I never thought I could call him "Daddy" again, but I did. Before I left, I told him, "Jesus loves you, Daddy, and I do too. I love you Daddy." I can still feel the hurt rise up into my face from my chest as I write these words. How is it that a child can love parents that have fallen so short in providing the love that child wants and needs? I thank God that though our parents may fail us, He never will. He is our Abba Father, our "Daddy God." God clearly spoke this to me after I got saved, and I have never felt alone since.

CR

My two sisters married their teen sweethearts and stayed in Alabama when my mama, her new man, my brother, and I moved to California. My sisters had not planned to marry that young. The oldest was barely

18 and the other was not yet 17 years old. They married because mama was leaving Alabama and they did not want to leave.

The trip to California was not what I had hoped for. After my step-daddy left I hoped to have a better life with my mama, but she quickly changed and I didn't feel that I knew her anymore. I didn't understand what she was thinking, and she wouldn't talk to me about any of it. She expected me to understand, but I didn't. I was a young girl about to grow up very fast.

Chapter Six: Growing Up Too Fast

With my step-daddy gone, I thought things would be different with my mama. I was willing to forget how she let our step-daddy treat us all those years if I could have a decent relationship with her after he left. It never happened. My mama was trying to find love that only God could give her. She was trying to fill a void that only He could fill.

The next year was a very hard year for me. I learned to try to make the best of things, which usually meant going along with things to keep peace. Mama and her new man separated not long after we got to California. She seemed to be very unhappy, going out and drinking more than she ever had. I had more responsibility than ever. I was always expected to keep all the kids while my mama and her friends went out to party. I was very lonely and unhappy.

At the age of sixteen I began to drink alcohol to be "grown up" and a part of my mama's life. A guy that my mama and her friends partied with started showing me some attention, and I ate it up. I now know that I was just trying to fill the void of a father's love with any attention that I could get. That relationship didn't last long. It ended one night when I walked in to see my mama with this guy that was suppose to be coming over to see me. I was so shocked to see the smile on my mama's face. I was so hurt and confused. At that moment, I lost all trust and hope in everyone and everything. I found all of the pain killers that mama had in the house and took them. I just didn't want to feel anything anymore.

I was sick and scared at the hospital, but I was afraid that if I told them the real reason I took the pills—the way it was at home—they would take my little brother and me away from my mama. I did not want to cause my little brother any more pain than he already had after being moved away from his two other sisters and losing his daddy. So, I just let them all believe what they wanted to.

I knew our mama was the only thing my little brother had. He was very close to her and clung to her all of the time. It was always hard on him when my mama would go out all night. As she would be walking out of the door, she would tell me to hold him down until she could get away because he would cry and beg and run after her. He would scream and kick and tear my clothes trying to get to her. I would have scratch marks all over my neck and arms and tears burning in my eyes for him. I would be so frustrated at Mama. I knew that she was not happy, but neither were we. We wanted her to stay with us so that we could be a family as best we could.

CR

All of the things that I have experienced in my life have molded me and made me into the person that I am today. Those experiences have made me the mother and the wife that I have become. I have heard people use the excuse that their mother or father were not good parents, therefore they themselves could not be a good parent. I think this is left up to the person. You have to decide for yourself that you *want* to be a good parent, and then find out *how* to become a good parent if you did not have an example to follow. You have to *want* to be a better person. You can not blame your faults and failures on anyone else.

We are all products of our childhood, but we can learn from the hurts and disappointments in our lives to change and improve. I strive daily to be a good wife and mama, but I don't have to do it alone. God's Word is there to help me and his Holy Spirit is there to guide me. He is there for you, too.

God would have helped Mama if she would have asked. My mama tells us today that she raised us the best way that she could. I guess that is true—it was the best way that *she alone* could have raised us, but not the best way that she could have raised us *with God's help*. As parents we need to realize that our children did not ask to be born, and our life should be about our children when we bring them into this world. Our children belong to God and He expects us to love them like He loves us. He will help us to raise them if we simply ask.

CR

My life at sixteen years old was a constant emotional battle. I helped to clean and do laundry as well as working a waitress job, but we still never seemed to have enough. Sometimes it all got to be too much. I did some things that I should not have. I skipped school on a couple of occasions and hung out with the wrong people.

When I was around my mama and her friends and family, I would drink alcohol when it was offered to me just to fit in and forget for awhile. I didn't need to drink after meeting my Eddie, however. He made me happy and gave me something to look forward to. God brought my Eddie into my life when I didn't think I wanted to live anymore. God knew that I was just a scared, hurt, and confused little girl. He knew that I needed my Eddie.

When Eddie came into my life I thought he was too good to be true. The first time I saw him he was working under the hood of his car. I was taken by him when he rose up and looked into my eyes with his big, brown, puppy-dog eyes. He was gorgeous then and still is. My Eddie would become my best friend, husband, and minister.

∞

I scared Eddie to death when I first began to come around. He lived across the street from me and I used every excuse I could think of to go to his house. He caught on very quickly. He began to watch for me and make himself available to talk to me, though he wasn't quite sure at first if he should. He was 23 years old and I was only 16. He had just gotten out of the Army, after serving six years, and had never met anyone that he thought he could marry and have a family with.

In spite of warnings from his big brothers, disapproving looks from everyone, and my mama's strict rules, Eddie decided to date me anyway. Boy, I am glad he did. Twenty-five years later and I am still taken by him!

Eddie and I began to see each other every chance we had. I had a little waitress job after school and on the weekends, so Eddie would pick me up from work and would sit with me while I watched my brother for my mama. My mama would not let us date and did not like Eddie coming over to see me. She could not believe that he was willing to simply hang out with my brother and me, and frequently told me as much.

Eddie could do anything he wanted, but he chose to be with me and my little brother. My mama told me I was crazy to think that I was the only one he was seeing. She had never met a real man like Eddie. I always gave Mama all of the money that I made at my little waitress job and tried to do everything she told me to so that I could see Eddie. Eddie was very quiet and well-mannered and did what she expected of him. He made my little brother's and my life a little better by spending that time with us.

CR

I guess my mama got tired of living in California, because she soon decided that she would move back to Alabama. After only five months of seeing each other, my mother gave Eddie and me the option to marry or to never see each other again. She didn't have room for me in her life anymore. She didn't have room for me in the car that she and five other people took back to Alabama.

I was scared to death when Eddie proposed to me on a dock under a beautiful sunset, but there was no way that I could lose the best thing that had ever happened to me. He promised that I would get to finish school because he knew how important it was to me. He assured me that he would take care of me. He knew that I was very young and scared, but he was too.

My mama took us just across the border into Mexico so that Eddie and I could get married. We spent the whole day there trying to figure out how to get married quickly so that my mama could leave. I felt like everything was all wrong, and I was angry at my mama for the way she was handling things. This was supposed to be an important time for me, and instead it felt wrong and rushed.

I was not happy, but I had learned a long time ago to make the best of things and to be happy anyway. I was so angry that I had a hard time looking Mama in the face that day. It was even harder to look at her and tell her good-bye when she and my little brother left for Alabama. Mama did manage to see Eddie and I married before she left. We were married at sunset, the same time of day that Eddie proposed. We finally found a little wedding chapel and a minister willing to marry us just across the border of Arizona. At the age of sixteen, in a little wedding chapel in Yuma, Arizona, without wedding rings or a wedding dress, I became a wife.

My mama left behind a little girl that had been forced to grow up without ever having the relationship with her mama that she wanted and needed. I was now a married woman about to start my own life and family. God brought Eddie to me and was looking out for me when I did not know it. He was in control of both mine and Eddie's lives from the beginning, and we didn't even know Him.

Chapter Seven: Family

Eddie and I were both sinners when we got married, but we tried to live a better life than what I had lived at home. The first year of our marriage was very special. We both worked to pay for our little studio apartment in Reseda, California, and spent all of our free time together. We had a wonderful time during our first year of marriage. We were married for a year and a half when I became pregnant with our first child. I was only eighteen years old, but had become an excited expecting mother as well as a wife. I was very happy, but I began to miss my family terribly. I wanted to go back home to Alabama, and Eddie agreed for us to go.

After two years and two months of marriage, I gave birth to our first child, our beautiful daughter, Le'Anne. We decided to go to a little church where some friends invited us, trying to "straighten up and live right." We felt then like it was the right thing to do for our child and ourselves, but had no idea what we were doing or how to do it. We both just prayed silently in our pew and tried to do what we thought was right for our little family.

CR

I was disappointed when I began to realize that things were not any better with my mama. She still didn't have room in her life for me, or my new baby. I finally realized that for two people to have a healthy relationship they both have to want it, and my Mama didn't want it. I was still the outsider with my two sisters and I would always be the different one. They thought that I was too religious because I wanted a better life than what they were living. I really wasn't that "religious" then. I didn't know much of anything about the Word of God. I didn't really know God; I just knew about Him.

This is a part of my life that is hard to share, but I know that I must if I am going to minister to people. The truth is that Eddie and I tried to be good and go to church, but we slowly slipped into a life that was not pleasing to God. We now realize that it was because we were never discipled. We had never really gotten to know Jesus. He had not truly become everything to us.

We never really became part of the church or fellowshipped with them. They didn't fellowship with us outside of church, and we had no family in church. There were not many evangelists on T.V. back then. Even if there were, we didn't have a television. It didn't take long before I was trying to be around my mama and sisters again. I am not making excuses for us. I just feel that we didn't truly give Jesus our whole heart, so it was easy to slip back into our old lives again. It is so very important for the church to disciple new Christians and to reach out to visitors. Bringing them into the church body will help them to become part of the family of God.

CR

I turned 21 and thought I was grown. I made Eddie take me out to the bars where my mama and sisters were. I was trying to be a part of their lives. I danced like Mama and drank like Mama, simply to be with her. It was not long before I became completely disgusted with myself. Although I loved Eddie and our little girl, I was trying to find happiness in everything and any person that I could. I was trying to find love and fulfillment in things that would never bring it. I was trying desperately to ignore the hurt and disappointments I had inside. I was trying to be someone that I was not.

Eddie had always done everything I asked him to. When I wanted to go out to party, he took me. He never wanted to go. He was happy just sitting at home drinking his beer and hiding his pain from his own hurts and disappointments in life, but I wanted to go out and I knew that he would do what ever I wanted him to. Women need to be very careful when it comes to manipulation. Our husbands love us and will do anything to please us. What we manipulate them to do will never turn out for good. A woman of God should never manipulate her husband. Of course, at that time, I was far from being a woman of God.

I began to see my mother in me and it scared me. If my siblings or I ever questioned anything our Mama did, she would say, "This is my life and I am going to live it like I want to." I questioned in my heart that if it was her life we were all living, then why had "her life" affected mine so much? The fact is that our own lives are never the only ones we affect. Our lives are not just about ourselves, but about our spouse, our children, and everyone around us. We affect others everyday.

☙

At the age of 21 I was miserable. I began to look at my life and examined what it meant. Deep down inside I had always felt that there was much more in life than what I and my family had lived. I always wanted more education than what the rest of my family settled for. I wanted a better life than what we had growing up, and I wanted to be a better person than any of us had become, but I didn't know how to bring this about. I went back to school for a while trying to accomplish something with my life. Mama had warned me not to think more of myself than I should, but I have always felt that my family should have thought more of themselves than they did.

It hurt me that I did not have a healthy relationship with my family, but I realized that I would have to separate myself from them to find a better life. The separation happened slowly over the following years, and was very difficult for me. Now, years later, I still miss my family. I see them occasionally, but I am not really a part of their lives the way they are with each other. I love them and I want for them the same joy and peace that I have with my Jesus. I want them to have the kind of relationship with the Father that will help them to serve Him when the people they love fail them.

CR

When you know in your heart that God is your "Abba Father," your Daddy God, and you know that He will never forsake you or leave you, and I mean really know it, then all of Hell can break loose in your life and you will stand. He will be there when no one else will. He gives you a purpose, and no matter what comes against you in life, you can keep pushing on because you know that His will for you is the most important thing in life. You know this is true because He was there when you went through hard times, and He brought you through.

God knows this about us. He knows that bringing us through the hard times is what convinces us that He loves us. There have been times that I would fret about situations, and then I would repent for fretting. After repenting I would fret some more. God in all of His goodness would then turn things around for me just to show me that He loves me and cares about everything that I go through.

It is then, when He turns things around for me and makes everything alright, that my heart leaps and soars with love and admiration and I know that He loves me. God makes us stronger and able to help others through hard times because we can tell them to hang on, stand, and trust Him to move in their situation. He loves to do for us if we will just let Him.

CB

Because I didn't have the family I wanted growing up, I decided to search out the family that I had never met. I decided to find my real daddy's family. One day I bravely approached my real daddy's father, my grandfather. I announced to him that I was the daughter of his deceased son. It was an awkward moment, and I cannot remember everything said. I was so nervous I stood shaking all over, afraid of being rejected.

I remember my grandfather asking me what it was that I had in mind in coming to visit him. I told him that I only wanted to meet him. Although my grandfather admitted that he believed I was his grandchild and that he could see his son in me, he also told me, "I heard an old black preacher say one time, 'Mama's baby, Papa's

61

maybe'." He began saying that a lot of time had gone by since his son had died, but I didn't hear the rest of what he had to say because I felt a sudden rush of hurt and rejection and numbness all over.

I turned and walked as quickly as I could to my car while he called out to me "Wait, don't go." Looking through tears, I could see him in my rearview mirror watching me drive away. I wish I had not walked away. I was running like I always had. I never saw him again.

The desire to know and be a part of my real daddy's family ended with the death of my grandfather. His obituary was read at his funeral. In the obituary, his deceased son—my real daddy—had a daughter mentioned. It was not me, but another daughter. The family knew that this daughter was illegitimately born, just as I was, but acknowledged her nonetheless. The family also knew about a third illegitimate daughter who had spent time with the family, as the mentioned daughter had, but like me, she was not mentioned in the obituary. The only daughter mentioned had a mother that was a "somebody" and was "in" with the family. The mentioned daughter was accepted into the family though her mother had never married our daddy.

The daughter mentioned in my grandfather's obituary had access that I did not have. My real daddy never married, so these two daughters and me, as well as any other children that he might have fathered, were all born illegitimately. One daughter just happened to have "access" into the family.

I know that you know where I am going with all of this! You and I have "access" to our Father's family through his son, Jesus. Wow, I felt the power when I wrote that! We are all a "somebody" in His family! Yes Ma'am I am! Yes Ma'am you am! I know that's not correct English, but it sounds good anyway!

CR

With the death of my grandfather I felt finality to my childhood, as if a door was slammed closed forever. All I had were the dreams I made up in my head as a child of what it could have been like if my daddy had lived. All I had was a picture I obtained on my own of the man who fathered me, but was never my daddy.

I shook all over as I sat through the reading of my grandfather's obituary. They read the names of the legitimate grandchildren and told of the family memories at the family house. I watched as my grandfather's legitimate family was seated up front in their proper place. I shook while their eyes avoided mine. I had no place there; no business there. I stopped shaking when my Heavenly father whispered, "Baby, don't you worry, you are counted in my family and you have a seat with me." He spoke so loudly and authoritatively to my heart, "You are mine!"

My Abba Father has taken me and made me his little girl now. If you are fatherless, let Him make you His child and see if He is not better than any earthly daddy could ever be. God wants to have a Father-and-Child relationship with us. I have not had that kind of relationship with an earthly father, so God had to teach me how to have it with Him. He loves us more than any earthly father or mother could. He will receive us just as we are, but He loves us too much to leave us that way.

God has healed me of that little girl hurt caused by the father and family that I grew up with and by my real father's family. I would now rather have people see Jesus in me than the features that I possess of my real father's family. I know that God has worked everything for my good and He will do the same for you, too.

I love the story of Joseph in Genesis. I love verse 20 in Chapter 50 where Joseph proclaims, "but God meant it unto good, to bring to pass, as it is this day…" (KJV). God showed me, through the writing of this book, that in all of our lives He meant it unto good, to bring to pass, as it is this day! I know God probably would have liked things to have been better for me and for you, but He will cause it all to be for good anyway! So, if I had to do it all over again and everything had to be the way it was for me to be where I am today, to be the person that I am today, then I would not change a thing.

Chapter Eight: The Holy Spirit

Eddie and I had been married for six-and-a-half years when I felt God pulling at my heart. I know He must have had His hand over us, because we both drank a lot in those days, trying to manage the hurt and disappointments in our lives. Eddie was very quiet when I told him that I wanted to straighten our lives out. I wanted to be a good family and live the way I knew in my heart that we should. I knew Eddie wanted this as well. He just didn't know how to do it.

At this point in our lives we had our second child, our first son, Jimmie. We were both so proud of Jimmie. Eddie loved his son and wanted the best for both of his children. He knew how to work and provide for them, but he didn't know how to become the man they needed him to be. He shared with me later that he didn't think God would give him another chance.

Eddie had his problems, but he handled them quietly and kept them all inside. I never knew what he was thinking, and he did not talk with me much. We had almost begun living in our own little separate worlds. I hated the people that Eddie and I had become. I didn't want our lives to slip by, and I didn't want our lives to become the way my life was growing up. I didn't know it then, but this was the Holy Spirit pulling at my heart and calling me to Him.

That pulling at my heart was very strong one day when Eddie, our two children, and I were at my sister's house. I was lying on my sister's bed singing my son Jimmie to sleep. I listened to my husband trying to laugh and talk with the rest of my family in the kitchen. I was feeling a void and I wanted my children to have a better childhood than what I had. I did not want them to grow up seeing Eddie and me drinking and wasting our lives. I felt the same in my heart as I had when I was eight years old in that little bed. I felt a deep calling in my heart to repent and walk with God. I was hungry for a better life that I knew only God could give. I felt desperate yet excited at the prospect of a new life.

My minister to be, my husband, was sitting at the table at my sister's house feeling just as miserable as I was. He had always worked hard, but never had a particular career in mind. He felt uncertain of where his life was going. We now know this was because his calling was to be a Minister.

I made up my mind that day to do something about our lives. I knew that my neighbor was a Christian and that she went to church, so I left a note on her door and asked her if I could go to church with her. It is not often that someone leaves a note on your door asking to go to church with you, so she knew I was desperate.

That night, Eddie and I lay in bed and talked about what we wanted for our lives. He cried big 'ole tears that formed puddles in his ears when I asked him if I could go to church with my neighbor. He replied, "Yeah baby, maybe you can bring something back for me." I did bring something back for him—a brand new wife and the hope of salvation!

◌ℜ

I went to church on a Wednesday night and they were having an annual business meeting, of all things. I got saved after that meeting at an empty altar with just me and God. I didn't know that God wanted me, an illegitimate little girl that tried everything on this earth to make myself feel worthy. I was disgusted with myself, but He made me feel clean and worthy and that I was a "somebody." I was His child now!

Eddie went to church with me on the following Sunday, and he got saved. We were saved for only two weeks when we went to a revival and were filled with the Holy Spirit. This made the difference in our ability to stand in our Christian walk when we did not have that ability before. Having the Holy Spirit has helped us to stand for eighteen years when we might otherwise have fallen away.

The first night of the revival I didn't go up to the altar because I was scared and I expected God to call me up there. I left disappointed that night, but I went back the next night and marched myself up to that altar just like the determined little girl that I have always been. Let me tell you, God met me there and filled me generously with his Holy Spirit.

CB

I know some Christians feel that we are filled with the Holy Spirit when we are saved. Acts 1:4-5 tells us that Jesus "commanded them that they should not depart from Jerusalem, but wait for the promise of the Father, which, *saith he,* ye have heard of me. For John truly baptized with water; but ye shall be baptized with the Holy Ghost not many days hence." I love what verse eight says, "But ye shall receive power, after that the Holy Ghost is come upon you: and ye shall be witnesses unto me." This is what has helped Eddie and me to stand and what has drawn us back to the Lord when we would get discouraged.

More verses to read are Acts 8:12-17. First the followers believed, then were baptized in water, and then baptized in the Holy Ghost. You first believe on the name of Jesus, but the baptism of water or the baptism in the Holy Ghost can come in any order. If a person dies before being baptized in water or in the Holy Ghost, they can still enter into Heaven if they have accepted Jesus as their personal Savior before death. However, we are to be baptized in water in obedience to the Word, and in the Holy Ghost to "receive power."

CR

Our determination and faith moves God. He will never fail us, and He will always meet us half-way. When we take steps forward, He takes just as many to meet us in our path. I didn't know this the night I headed to the altar, but Eddie had gone up right behind me and met with the Holy Spirit as well.

The preacher at that revival preached the power of God into our lives. We went to church every time the doors were open, learning about deliverance and walking with God in victory. We prayed for deliverance from the things in our lives that kept us from serving Him. We prayed for deliverance from things in our childhood and our past and were set free from bondage that was holding us down from serving God.

This did not happen in one night. Eddie and I had to walk it out. God lead us by the hand and gently dealt with us day by day. There are things from our past that God will use to make us strong and determined, but there are also things that the Devil will use to destroy us unless we let God deliver us from them. We are delivered by the preaching of the Word and by then responding to the altar call after the Word is preached. It is wonderful how God gives a preacher the Word for the hour and then he will meet us in the altars to complete the work. This is how we grow; we respond to the Word and let the Holy Spirit perform the work in us as we submit to His drawing.

Your hunger for the things of God determines how fast you will grow. I wanted to grow to be what God wanted me to be, but there were times that I thought my heart would break first. I remember on one particular occasion going into my room and throwing myself on my bed. I cried out to God that he might as well give up on me because I could not be a Minister's wife or even a good Christian. If I have ever heard God before in my life, I heard Him that day. He said, "Lesia, it's not anything you and I can't work through." Joy filled my soul. Whenever I get to my lowest, He is always there to help me.

☙

I have seen minister's wives sit in the back of the church hiding out from the ministry because of discouragement. They leave their husband's side, crippling his ministry. My sweet husband has encouraged me during times of discouragement by telling me that he could not be effective in the ministry without me. He helps me to see that we truly are a team in the ministry and it is important for me to remain by his side and not run and hide, leaving him standing alone and incomplete.

Here is a poem that I once read on the back of a church bulletin.

There is one person in our church,
who knows our pastor's life,
Who weeps and smiles and prays with him
and that's the pastor's wife.
The crowd had seen him in his strength
when wielding God's sharp sword,
As underneath God's banner's folds
he faced the devil's horde.
But deep within her heart she knows
that scarce an hour before,
She helped him pray the glory down
behind the closet door.
She's heard him groaning in his soul
when bitter raged the strife,
As, hand in hand, she knelt with him
for she's the pastor's wife!
You tell your tales of prophets brave
who marched across the world,
And changed the course of history
by burning words they hurled,
And I will tell how back of each
some woman lived her life;
Who wept with him and smiled with him;
she was the pastor's wife!

Author Unknown

Chapter Nine: The Minister's Wife

It was not long after we were saved and Spirit-filled that Eddie felt the call on his life to preach. This in itself was a miracle. Before we were saved, Eddie was a shy, quiet man. You never heard much from him unless he was drinking a beer. Even after we were saved, Eddie had problems looking the cashier in the face at McDonald's long enough to order food. He never offered anything to a conversation unless he was asked a question, and then he used as few words as possible. To get up in front of a church and preach God's Word was definitely going to take the Anointing of God.

So now, I was to become a preacher's wife. I thought I could do it, but boy, did we both have some things to learn! God knew we would need to be filled with his Holy Spirit to be able to survive the making of a minister and his wife. I felt like Eddie and I could do anything for

God. We were saved, filled with the Spirit of God, and ready to do whatever God wanted us to do. The first thing we had to do was trust God in the financial mess we landed in right after we were saved. Eddie had to quit his job working with some close friends because after we were saved we no longer had anything in common with them. We were excited about being saved and wanted the same for our friends, but they wanted no part of it. We could no longer do the things we did with them before we were saved, nor did we want to. They could not understand what had happened in us. Eddie had to take a low-paying job for awhile. We had to learn to trust God for our lives.

Because of our financial situation, we did not have a vehicle for the first year that we were saved. We had to depend on the people of the church for a ride to church services. We had to walk to the store to get groceries. When we made a grocery run, Eddie and I would have to carry groceries and our two children, so we had to make several trips a week. My sweet Eddie would also walk to work most of the time, three miles there and three miles back. He only made $4.25 an hour working at the local lumber mill, and was exposed to unbearable heat and cold at times. He was a hard worker and very faithful. He kept a good attitude and let Jesus beam from him. Everyone at his job knew that he was a Godly man, and he ministered his new love of Jesus to any that would listen.

Things were hard while Eddie was only making $4.25 an hour. We had to live by faith. I remember having to borrow toilet paper until payday. Eddie and I did without to feed our two children and to pay the rent, which was usually paid in halves—half one week and half the next week. The last two weeks' paychecks would pay the light bill, water bill, and groceries. It was hard, but we were happy and determined to hang in there.

There were some insinuations made about our financial situation by people in our church back then. The general belief was that to be considered favored of God and blessed, one owned a lot of material things. If you didn't have those material things, God must have a problem with you. We know that this is not true. Sometimes God allows us to go through things to mature us and cause us to have faith. 1 Peter 5:10 says, "But the God of all grace, who hath called us unto his eternal glory by Christ Jesus, after that ye have suffered a while, make you perfect, establish, strengthen, settle you."(KJV)

We were hurt by comments made by the very ones that should have been encouraging us, which was the family of God. We missed opportunities for financial gain and spiritual growth from the actions of these very ones that should have been looking out for us. Those first few years were hard, but necessary for our spiritual growth.

After the first year we were saved we received an income tax refund and began to look for a car. We went about two weeks and could not find anything that we could get with $900, the amount of money we had after we faithfully paid our tithe of $100 from the $1,000 tax refund. One day, the Lord began to deal with me. He told me that whatever Eddie decided to do with the money, I was to agree with him and support him as my head that God had placed over me. I was learning what it meant to be a Godly woman. I was already living a different life than how I was raised.

Eddie never tried to take advantage of the honor of being the head of the house and family. He always talked with me and I trusted him and God. When Eddie came home and told me he had to give our money away, the very money we were to use to buy a car, I could do nothing but agree. It really was not hard for me because I was excited to see God do something in our lives. We had learned that when you obey

God, He will move on your behalf and take care of you. It was exciting!

The situation with our money for the car was between Eddie and God. God had dealt with Eddie because of a comment he had made to a fellow employee concerning faith. He and the co-worker had been listening to a local radio station while working that day. The man on the radio was begging people to send in their money, and shaming them if they did not. Eddie made the comment that the man on the radio needed to have faith in God to provide for his needs, not get on the radio day after day speaking desperately and becoming angry that people did not send money to his station.

Well, Eddie was right, but God chose this situation to allow the Devil and all of Hell to witness His son, Eddie, in complete obedience to Him. God told Eddie to give his money to this desperate-sounding man on the radio, and asked Eddie to trust Him for his car! Eddie came home that day and did not even look at me. He headed for the shower, and I could hear him praying. He not only had to borrow a truck to take the money to the man at the radio station, but also had to convince his little wife (that had been traveling on foot everywhere with him) that God told him to do this.

I had already heard from God that day in my daily time with Him, so I took the opportunity God was giving me to build up my man of God by submitting under his authority and being in agreement with him. While God was making Eddie His minister, he was making me His minister's wife.

Eddie didn't waste any time. He went straight to the station, walked in, handed the money to the man, and said, "God told me to give this to you." The man had been in his office with a few other people praying and believing God for the money. Eddie did not tell him his name. He just walked out, went home, and waited on God.

Two weeks later, the man that owned the truck Eddie borrowed to deliver the money to the radio station stood in our living room and handed Eddie the keys to a car for our family. This man had learned something from Eddie. God used this man to bless Eddie, and I believe that Eddie blessed that man as well. I know it was very hard for Eddie to receive the car from the man, but it did a great thing in Eddie. He learned that we have to receive from God the way God chooses to bless, and we also have to let Him have His way with our hearts and lives.

We counted ourselves blessed to be chosen to go through the fire. Things began to get better for us. I got a job working at night so that one of us would always be with our children. I would miss Eddie and the children, and they would miss me, but we were willing to do what we had to. Le'Anne was five and Jimmie was about eighteen months old. It was hard for them to be without me at night. Le'Anne would get my nightgown from my room so that she could smell me as she fell to sleep. It would always break my heart to see their little faces pressed against the windowpane, watching me as I left for work.

❦

Eddie and I both worked jobs and stayed faithful to our church, striving to find our purpose in God's Kingdom. We began ministering to the people in our community. Our church was located in a community with project housing. We loved those people and they loved us. We opened our hearts and lives to women who had illegitimate children, as well as to children who were being raised by their grandparents.

Most of the women we visited were dealing drugs and prostituting while living on welfare in the projects. Eddie and I would go out to visit them at least twice a week and invite them to church. We ministered to men that would gather around a fire in a barrel to stay warm while they drank their whiskey. Most of the men in that community did not work to support the women and children. We saw a lot of sad things that touched our hearts and moved us to minister to the needs around us.

The body needs to be fed just as the soul does. We saw many children living in poverty worse than what we lived in. I still don't know how we made it back then. We had very little, but we were always able to help when we needed to. God always supplies.

We bused the children we visited to church and sometimes the mothers would come. They never stayed long. Eddie and I did our best to make them feel at home, but we had a hard time getting people in the church to stay faithful in helping us. They would help for a while, but would soon grow tired of it. It was hard when we realized that most of our church body did not have the same vision that we had for the kids living in the projects. This included the pastors. The kind of congregation that our church body wanted was not the kind we were bringing in. My heart has always been with the people that others do not want to be bothered with: the poor, illegitimate, disabled, and hurting.

CƠ

As we grew in the Lord, we began to go through some of the things that would mold us and make us into vessels that God can use in the ministry. Eddie preaches today how God encouraged him to be part of the praise and worship team at church before he was able to stand up and preach to a congregation. God knew that Eddie needed practice being in front of a church body.

The Devil knew that if he could stop Eddie here, he would never preach the gospel. Eddie struggled every time that he got on the stage, but he kept going up there. Although he has a beautiful voice, Eddie struggled with timing and remembering words to songs. He could not look at the congregation while he sang, so he sang to the ceiling and the walls.

Eddie also battled uncomfortable situations with one of the members of the worship team. We didn't know it then, but we have now learned that though people go to church, they are not always where they need to be with God. Eddie battled a situation with a woman on the worship team flirting relentlessly with him. He tried desperately to avoid the situation, and would turn red from embarrassment in front of the whole congregation.

We needed help with this problem, but no one in leadership wanted to deal with it. Today's Church allows the Devil to take far too much ground. We have to deal with situations in the church instead of letting those situations destroy what God is trying to build. When those in leadership are not where they need to be in their relationship with the Lord, the Devil can come in and make the church body look like fools. Eddie and I have seen churches destroyed because of this very reason.

☙

I didn't want anything to hinder what God was trying to do in Eddie's life. I could see that Eddie was really beginning to grow in the Lord. We turned to the Word of God to deal with our problem the way the Word says to deal with situations: in love and confrontation. We were young Christians and had to fervently pray and ask for God's help. God alone has the ability to deal with people. He may use us, but learn this simple thing now: if God chooses to use you to deal with a person, he will let you know. Be sure it's God or you could get chewed up and spit out.

During the time Eddie and I were dealing with our problem, I found myself talking with a male co-worker about the frustrations and disappointments that I was facing. He always seemed to be there and ready to listen to me. Before I knew it, he began to try to be what Eddie was supposed to be for me. You see how sneaky the Devil is? Beware, women of God, because he will come in any way that we let him. I tell my teenage boys today, "The Devil is not always going to show up at the foot of your bed—he comes in sneaky ways!" The good news is that we have the Holy Spirit looking out for us, ready to intervene when the Devil comes in trying to destroy our lives.

❧

The word Christian means "Christ-like." When Christians refuse to be Christ-like, we have to let God handle them and continue to be Christ-like ourselves. God showed me that, in the situation with the woman flirting with my husband, I needed to be bold as a lion, but gentle as a dove. Praise God, He also showed me that I had every right to tell any woman who touched my man to keep her hands off, and believe me, I will! However, so far I haven't had to. This type of situation has never happened again.

Chapter Ten: The Ministry

In the seventh year of our salvation, the Lord led us to be a part of a church that had a wonderful praise and worship service. It was at this time that God healed me and restored my broken spirit. It was a time of rest and revival for me. At this point in my life, all I wanted was to be a good wife and mother, and to please God.

I worked in the church and obeyed the spirit of God when he chose to use me in the services. God began to use me to pray for others. Up until this point, it seemed that I was always in the altars trying to get myself straight. I now know that when you go through trials and hurts, and you see God bring you through, it gives you the faith to pray for others. God began to use me to intercede in the Spirit for His people after He ministered to my life.

I once heard a pastor tell a story about ministry. The pastor said he went to visit a man that was an amputee. This man had become bitter and would not go to church, or anywhere else for that matter. He just sat at home because he hated the artificial leg that he had been fitted with. The man would not listen to reasoning or receive any encouragement. When the pastor finally talked this man into going to visit his doctor to see what could be done, the man explained his bitterness to the doctor. The doctor listened patiently until the man had let all the frustration and anger pour out of him. When the man was finished, the doctor smiled sweetly and raised the leg of his trousers to reveal his own artificial leg. God used that doctor to minister to the man when no one else could.

CR

After the birth of our third and last child, Jonathan, whose name means the "gift of the Lord," I began having some back problems from degenerative disk disease. Little did I know, this would be the beginning of ten years of one problem after another in my body.

After having the first two of three back surgeries, I spent a lot of time alone while Eddie was at work and the children were at school. It was just me and little Jon-Jon. I lived in a lot of pain and frustration. I could not recover from the back surgeries or handle the pain.

The doctors said I would continually get worse and would have to live on medication to control the pain, inflammation, and swelling, and that I would eventually be debilitated. I refused to accept that. I literally spent time with my face in the carpet before God. Eddie felt that he was ready to step out into the ministry, and I wanted to be able to stand by his side. I put all of my faith in God for my healing.

I began to spend more time in God's Word. I could see God's anointing on Eddie to preach and I felt Him preparing me to be by Eddie's side in the altars. I loved to pray for people with pain in their hearts and in their bodies. I don't know which pain is worse. I think both hurt just as much. I have been there, just as most of you have.

Eddie was almost finished with his ministerial studies, and I went back to our community college to finish my education. I wanted to be equipped to help Eddie in the administrative aspect of the ministry.

CR

The full-time ministry didn't come as quickly as we thought it would, or as quickly as we wanted it to. We were discouraged when opportunities didn't arise where we were living, so we began searching for a place to continue to grow and minister. We moved our family to a different area in hopes of finding the right church. We visited different churches and saw more "stuff" than what we wanted to. Because we took our eyes off of God and placed them on people, we soon became disappointed and frustrated.

We couldn't find the right church for our family, so for a while we didn't go anywhere. It was not long before we got into trouble spiritually. It was in those times that our children got to see that Daddy and Mama, the preacher and his wife, were not perfect. They saw that we need His mercy and grace that is new everyday, just like everyone else.

It is so important to find the church that God wants you to be a part of and not jump around from church to church. We learned this the hard way. We learned that there are going to be some "real" Christians and some "not so real" Christians in any church, and there will always be "stuff." God was trying to make us see that we had to get past the "stuff." He showed us that we were at a dangerous place in our hearts and lives. He showed us that there will always be some things about a church that won't be exactly what we think they should be. He showed us that we weren't completely what we should be either, and that this was actually the problem. The problem was never people and the church, but us. In His mercy and grace, He lovingly said, "I am still here. I never left you or gave up on you."

As I think back, it seems that we learned *everything* the hard way. There were times when we felt we could never be what God needed us to be. Years later we realized that there will be hurting people coming into the church in the last days, and these people need to be ministered to by someone that has been in their shoes. Bishop T.D. Jakes once preached that it took him "ten years to go through what only took 40 minutes to preach!" Listening to Bishop Jakes has encouraged Eddie and me and helped us to realize that there was a reason for us to go through what we have. We appreciate his ministry and the honesty that is revealed in his preaching.

Someone else that my husband and I love is Joyce Meyer. Joyce preaches with such honesty and realness. I appreciate that about her. She does not let you feel sorry for yourself but instead encourages you to get real with yourself so that God can use you to minister to others. Ministry has to be done with honesty and realness. Being phony does not minister to anyone.

CR

By the year 2000, we had been through a lot and began looking at where we were going. We knew it was forward, because the hunger for the things of God had taken its place far above anything that the Devil tried to throw at us. We knew it was time to shut the back door to our hearts that we had left cracked opened just in case we wanted to run out when it got too tough. We had finally gotten to the place where we knew we had to do God's will in our lives and trust God to take care of the rest. God is always right on time in our lives.

CR

A little country church that had been closed up asked us to come and pastor at this time. They did not know that we had almost closed the doors on our hearts just as they had closed the doors on their church. The church had all of about seventeen people, but that was all we needed. It was a renewing time for Eddie and me. It was pulpit time for Eddie. Every time he preached he got better, and the more he trusted God for the Word, the stronger the anointing was. God preached to him while Eddie preached to the people.

God used Eddie to stir a fire in those people and in us. When Eddie had to take a job that was shift-work, he gave up the church to a man that could be there on a regular basis. God was finished with us at that church, but He continued to put us under men of God that would give Eddie the opportunity to preach as we waited for the full-time ministry. I want to mention one man here. His name is Reverend Steve Pettis. Steve is the best friend that Eddie has ever had in the ministry. He shared his pulpit with Eddie, spent time with him, and encouraged him like no one else ever has. Steve preached with anointing and enriched our lives. We are so thankful for Steve and his wife, Regina, and for the investment that they made in our lives. They prayed with us through some of the hardest times we've faced.

One of these times was when I was still struggling with incredible back pain while working an office job. I suddenly became extremely sick with intestinal problems. In just a two-year period I had five major surgeries, with multiple procedures and tests.

Eddie and I both learned things through this time that strengthened us as ministers. Eddie grew spiritually in spite of the schedule he had to keep with his full-time job and the stress of helping his sick wife. He still found some time to preach and some time for the kids. He grew as he had to have faith while watching me go through all of the surgeries. I had to have faith to get through them. Our relationship was strengthened with each other and with God.

℞

I spent valuable time alone with God through that time. When it got tough, I would cry out to God and feel the Father literally snatch the Devil's hands off of me and run him out of the room. Bishop T.D. Jakes once preached that the Lord comes running to our aid in times of need, passionately encourages us not to give up, and assures us that He is not through with us yet. Bishop Jakes preached with a strong anointing of how the Lord loves us and how it hurts Him when we go through things in life. He preached that when we cry out to Jesus in desperation, He rushes to our side. We just have to cry out to Him. Cry out to Him when you think that you can't go on and when it looks like nothing is ever going to work out the way you have prayed. Begin to pray for His Will for your life instead of your will and you will begin to see some changes.

Sometimes when we pray we do not see and realize what is taking place in the spiritual realm. Rest assured that God hears us, and He puts things into action in our hearts and in our lives. Sometimes we think that if we don't see things actually happen, then nothing is happening, but just hold on! I can look back now and remember praying for changes in my heart and life; praying for a pure heart and mind and a strong body. I see the changes in my heart more than in my physical body, but I once heard someone say that this is because God is preparing us spiritually for the changes that He is about to make physically. I can't remember who said it, but I liked it!

ଔ

The desire Eddie and I had to be in full-time ministry was not ours originally, but put there in our hearts by the Father. It was His desire for us and He has brought it to pass in His time. While waiting for full-time ministry, we found peace when we began ministering for today and trusting God for tomorrow. We ministered in everyday life as the opportunity arose. We made ourselves available to God and He used us daily. There are a lot of hurting people that need to hear that Jesus loves them. We let them know that He has sent His Holy Spirit to guide and comfort them until He comes back to get us to be with Him forever. First Thessalonians 4:16-17 assures us of this, and verse

18 tells us to "comfort one another with these words." You need to know that He has a will for your life until that day.

At the end of the year of 2006, while praying for a new beginning for the year 2007, we were invited to a revival by our Sunday school teacher. Bill and Beni Johnson of Bethel Temple out of Redding, California, came to Mobile, Alabama, to minister. I went to the altar for prayer that night at the end of the service with more than healing for my body on my mind. I knew that Eddie and I were about to enter into full-time ministry. Eddie and I could feel it alive in our spirits like it was right on our heels and about to overtake us. I wanted to reach people and minister God's healing love to them in the way that I needed it. Brother Bill and his wife Beni prayed for me that night using my daughter Le'Anne to intercede for me. I received a miraculous healing in my body. Bill and Beni both prayed for our ministry before letting us go, and we were voted into our first church within two weeks.

My husband, Rev. Edward L. Jones, had become who he was always meant to be. He was so excited to be a pastor. One of the first things he preached was that the man is the head of the house and therefore it is his responsibility to live his life for the Lord and set an example for his household. He preached that the man must not only teach those in his house the Word of God, but live it before them and bring them up in it. Likewise, the wife has a responsibility to submit to her husband as her husband submits to God. She must be the wife and mother that the Word of God instructs her to be. Proverbs 31 is my favorite chapter for this instruction.

જી

My Eddie serves the Lord with passion. He has caused my heart to want to submit to him and to walk out our walk for the Lord together. He has finished raising me and has encouraged me to be all that I can be for God. I am the happiest woman alive. I have finally become who I was always meant to be: a minister's wife. Eddie has grown into a great man of God that has let God take complete control of his life. He is an anointed preacher, a wonderful husband, and a good father. He is a disciplined man of God.

Eddie has blessed me with life-giving words at the very times that I needed them the most. He spoke peace into my heart one day when he told me, "Lesia, yesterday is gone. Good or bad, it is gone. Today is what matters. You can have peace and happiness for today." He then continued, "You can be encouraged by remembering that tomorrow is untouched!" These words have helped me to leave the past in the past where it belongs. They have also helped me to remember that today is where I can make a difference and tomorrow is full of possibilities.

I want to pass those words on to you. I want you to know that yesterday is gone. Good or bad, it is gone. Today is what matters and you can have peace and joy for today by realizing that your Heavenly Father has a plan for your life. Today is where you can make a difference, if you submit your life totally to the Father and His will for your life. Be encouraged that tomorrow is untouched and full of possibilities. Everything God has done for me and through me, He can and will do for you. So, in the words of my husband, my preacher, "Don't settle for less than what He has for you."

Jimmie, Edward, Lesia, Jonathan & Le'Anne

www.ingramcontent.com/pod-product-compliance
Lightning Source LLC
Chambersburg PA
CBHW031326040426

42443CB00005B/226